You Know You've Been A Stay-At-Home Mom Too Long When....

BY
© JANICE HAAS & SALLY PESSIN
2004

D0008765

Published by Quixote Press

COVER DESIGN BY
Vicki Linden Beach

To David – for all you do
Evan and Jacob – you're the best
And for my mother
With love to you all
JH

For Andy and Eric – I love you guys!
SP

For David, Tyler, Eric, and Hannah
With love,
AA

INTRODUCTION

Although our book, **You Know You've Been A Stay-At-Home Mom Too Long When...** can be categorized as "light humor," underneath the one-liners, there is a deeper meaning. With this book, we pay homage to the stay-at-home mom, dad, or caregiver – that person who spends every waking minute with their child, giving so much of themselves all day, every day. It is not an easy job. It may be the most important job one will have; yet, it certainly does not get the respect it deserves.

As stay-at-home moms ourselves, we know that desperate feeling for some adult companionship, and at other times that strong desire for time alone. With this book, we're giving a huge high-five to our peers, those who put their careers on hold to raise their children, and to those who choose to be a stay-at-home mom for their career. It is a truly rewarding experience, yet it can be challenging at times. Our advice is to take some time for yourself and to take care of yourself, both physically and emotionally. Also, we suggest you seek out a network of friends in the same boat. There are so many "mom" groups out there that are not only fun, but will give you the conversation, support, and strength to do what you love and feel is right for your family. In the meantime, it is our hope that the humor in this book will help you through the rough patches and bring a smile to your face.

JH and SP

Acknowledgements

For our family and friends, thank you for your support, encouragement and for picking out the funny ones. Thanks to Marilyn and Bruce Carlson of Quixote Press for believing in us.

**You Know You've Been
A Stay-At-Home Mom Too Long When . . .**

———————————

All household decisions between you and your husband are now made by the Rock-Paper-Scissors method.

You think your minivan is SOOOOO cool.

You start twitching uncontrollably when someone refers to you as a housewife.

_____

*After convincing your
toddler to give up the bottle,
the pacifier, and Pull-Ups,
you feel well qualified to be
a hostage negotiator.*

. . . . .

Adjusting your child's car seat, you find
an M & M stuck underneath it from God
knows how long ago; you
EAT IT.

**You Know You've Been
A Stay-At-Home Mom Too Long When . . .**

Someone asks your age. Your reply: "516 months."

YOU ARE NO LONGER SURE WHETHER OR NOT THE FOLLOWING ARE ACTUAL WORDS: YUCKY, MUSHY, TUSHY, COOTIES, ICKY, AND GLOPPY.

The most loaded question your spouse asks you: "So what did you do today?"

You Know You've Been
A Stay-At-Home Mom Too Long When . . .

YOU CAN GET THROUGH A WEEK
USING SIX WORDS: CAREFUL,
SHARE, NO, CHEW, AIM AND WIPE.

* * * * *

*Your husband comes home
and you can't wait to show
him your biggest achievement
that day: a cool fort you
made out of sofa cushions.*

On a rainy day, you're walking, holding your Batman umbrella, talking with your friend, who's holding her Mickey Mouse umbrella and you think, "What happened to us?"

You Know You've Been
A Stay-At-Home Mom Too Long When . . .

_____

Your child is home sick from school. You've played Trouble, Bingo, Chinese checkers, regular checkers, Monopoly Jr., read sixteen books and watched *Rugrats*. It's now 9:48 A.M. You have ELEVEN more hours to go.

YOU START TO BELIEVE
JOHN EDWARD.

Your daily 43-second shower more closely resembles a hose-down.

You Know You've Been
A Stay-At-Home Mom Too Long When . . .

YOU REALIZE YOUR FRIENDS
ARE PAID HIGH SALARIES TO SIT
AT THEIR DESKS ALL DAY AND
E-MAIL YOU JOKES WHILE YOU
ARE HOME WIPING RUNNY
NOSES FOR FREE.

•   •   •   •   •

*The National Organization
for Women has revoked your
membership.*

YOU CAN'T GO TO THE BATHROOM WITHOUT THE DOOR OPENING AND A TINY VOICE CALLING, "MOMMY."

* * * * *

On your speed dial before you had kids: Victoria Secret catalog, Chinese carryout, Moviephone. On your speed dial now; Domino's, twelve babysitters, your pediatrician, and the emotional crisis hotline.

You Know You've Been
A Stay-At-Home Mom Too Long When . . .

The cashiers at Safeway see you so often, they give you an employee discount.

• • • • •

The only income you have to report this year is the $8.43 you netted from a lemonade stand you set up with your six-year-old.

You Know You've Been
A Stay-At-Home Mom Too Long When . . .

Craving adult companionship when Jehovah's Witnesses come calling, you not only open the door, you insist they stay for lunch.

The main topics of conversation at playgroup are:

a. Childbirth experiences
b. Hemorrhoids and that donut ring to sit on
c. How Tinky Winky's sex life should be a non-issue
d. How your sex life *is* a non-issue

The person you used to admire most: Mother Teresa; the person you now most admire: the individual who invented Velcro shoe straps.

• • • • •

Your working friends spend their lunch hour in restaurants with colleagues; you spend your lunch hour – wait a minute, what lunch hour????

You Know You've Been
A Stay-At-Home Mom Too Long When . . .

_____

Judging the best restaurants in town, you use these criteria...

a. They serve chicken fingers with fries.

b. They have connect-the-dot menus with *NEW* crayons.

c. There's a changing table in the bathroom.

All of your jeans have a hole in the knee.

You Know You've Been
A Stay-At-Home Mom Too Long When . . .

Your single sister talks of a great suspense movie that kept her hanging on the edge. You tell her that you really felt your heart racing during that last part of "Scooby Doo Where Are You?"

· · · · ·

You know every single Barbie ever made.

You Know You've Been
A Stay-At-Home Mom Too Long When . . .

YOU REALIZE THAT YOU DO THE
SAME JOB AS AN ILLEGAL ALIEN,
BUT THE ALIEN GETS PAID.

**Your five-year-old gives you a
manicure, and you think it looks
pretty good.**

Thanks to no second income, your
family's second car is a
riding mower.

YOUR EROTIC DREAMS OF BRAD
PITT AND TOM CRUISE HAVE BEEN
REPLACED BY APPEARANCES OF
YOUR CHILD'S PEDIATRICIAN.

* * * * *

**On Friday, you have to summon all
your willpower to resist committing
an act of violence after hearing your
husband say, "I really need some
time to myself this weekend."**

You can now distinguish between Burnt Sienna and Mahogany from the big Crayola crayon box.

• • • • •

You actually know which foreign country each nanny in the neighborhood is from.

You Know You've Been
A Stay-At-Home Mom Too Long When . . .

You finally have a reason to put on make-up and shave...annual Ob-Gyn visit!

Feng Shui for you is having an equal amount of Legos scattered throughout your house.

On your last visit to the doctor, a **CAT** scan revealed that due to a lack of adult interaction, you are technically brain dead.

You Know You've Been
A Stay-At-Home Mom Too Long When . . .

_____

A typical day looks like this...

Morning:
Buy SpongeBob pool shoes.
Buy light-up sneakers.
Buy glow-in-the-dark
underwear.

Afternoon:
Return SpongeBob pool shoes.
Return light-up sneakers.
Return glow-in-the-dark
underwear.

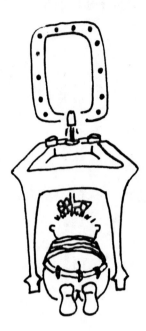

You slip a little Viagra into your plumber's coffee just to see what will happen.

You Know You've Been
A Stay-At-Home Mom Too Long When . . .

You have a major celebration: You no longer have to schlep that huge, ugly diaper bag around.

* * * * *

In their free time, your working friends are reading, *Who Moved My Cheese?* With your free time, you go to Chuck E. Cheese.

You Know You've Been
A Stay-At-Home Mom Too Long When . . .

Anne Heche's version of experimentation: sex with another woman. Your version of experimentation: substituting applesauce for butter in a brownie recipe.

THE COMIC STRIP, "BABY BLUES" IS TELLING YOUR LIFE STORY.

Your new favorite writing utensil is wide sidewalk chalk.

You Know You've Been
A Stay-At-Home Mom Too Long When . . .

_____

You are so out of touch with politics, you think that Bob Dole is still somewhere in Congress - the problem is, so does Bob Dole.

You received a Palm Pilot as a gift. You only use it to schedule your child's playdates.

"Hi, Honey, how was your day?" is replaced with, "Here, they're yours now!"

You Know You've Been
A Stay-At-Home Mom Too Long When . . .

_____

POP QUIZ #1

A Boppy is:

1. Hitting your misbehaving kid lightly over the head with a newspaper.
2. A circular pillow designed to lend support while nursing.
3. A euphemism for sex.

Meconium is:

1. A newly identified planet.
2. The black fecal matter your infant makes shortly after emerging from the womb.
3. The planned successor to the computer processing chip, Pentium.
4. A city in Iowa.

Impetigo is:

1. A bacterial skin infection.
2. A toy with small, brightly colored building blocks.
3. A new cocktail in hip bars in Manhattan.
4. A risqué Latin dance.

You are best known as:

1. The den mother for your son's cub scout troop.
2. The room parent in your kid's class.
3. The crazy woman on the block with the sticky house.

You Know You've Been
A Stay-At-Home Mom Too Long When . . .

_____

Children are a:

1. Joy to behold.
2. Way to ensure propagation of the species.
3. Wonderful form of birth control.

T.V. is:

1. A polluter of small minds.
2. The leading cause of obesity in American children.
3. A Godsend.

When your five-year-old asks you where babies come from, you tell him:

1. The stork.
2. Your doctor cut an enormous, painful hole in your belly, and now you have a huge ugly scar.
3. That he was delivered via the Heimlich Maneuver.
4. Go ask your dad.

Gourmet cooking to you is:

1. Concocting your own marinades.
2. Knowing that julienne is not a French girl's name, but rather a way to cut vegetables.
3. Not burning the Eggos.

You Know You've Been
A Stay-At-Home Mom Too Long When . . .

Due to your lack of sex drive, you let your husband subscribe to the Playboy Channel with the one condition that he makes no contact with the screen.

* * * * *

You no longer make meals for yourself. You just eat leftover table scraps.

...And you *enjoy* leftover table scraps.

You spend so much time driving your kids around that your backside has a permanent car logo impression from your seat.

You Know You've Been
A Stay-At-Home Mom Too Long When . . .

———————————

YOU'VE READ *GOOD NIGHT MOON*, *PAT THE BUNNY*, AND *HOP ON POP*, A GRAND TOTAL OF 2,867,924 TIMES.

You can now get a major hangover from five sips of a mimosa.

Your whole life (prior to kids), you HATED "toilet talk." Now, as your child sits on the potty, you get a play-by-play of the action and you think to yourself, "Isn't he the cutest?"

You're at the mall with your two-year-old because you need a battery for your watch. Cost of battery: $8. Cost of treats to get your child not to scream in the mall: $59.54. Cost of being able to go to the mall alone: priceless.

You Know You've Been
A Stay-At-Home Mom Too Long When . . .

You're pretty certain that even your dog is looking at you thinking, "When are you going to get a *real* job?"

* * * * *

You used to choose your cereal by the list of healthy ingredients. Now, it's either Lucky Charms or any box with a NASCAR prize inside.

You Know You've Been
A Stay-At-Home Mom Too Long When . . .

THE CABLE GUY SAYS HE CAN'T
MAKE IT UNTIL NEXT WEEK.
YOU PROMISE HIM AN
ICE CREAM TREAT IF HE'LL
COME SOONER.

*Desperate for some excitement,
you send a park full of nannies
scrambling by yelling, "INS!"*

Someone who has an office job asks
you, "What do you do all day with all
of that time?" You respond with,
"Besides sleeping with your husband?"

You realize that your hobbies have changed from tennis and skiing to sandcastles and bubble blowing.

YOU PONDER DEEP PHILOSOPHICAL QUESTIONS SUCH AS, "IF THEY CAN SEND A MAN TO THE MOON, WHY CAN'T THEY MAKE A THOMAS THE TRAIN SHOW WHERE THE TRAINS' MOUTHS MOVE?"

Your idea of a great shopping day is getting out of the store without buying Kit Kat bars, Fruit Roll-ups and Nerds.

* * * * *

You're on a family road trip. It's been hours. If you hear one more, "When are we going to be there?" someone is going out the window. Suddenly, God has delivered a miracle – A PLAYLAND MCDONALD'S!

You have eaten enough Pepperidge Farm
Goldfish to fill a Volkswagen; you are
way too in touch with your "inner pig."

Your kid's teacher asks you to chaperon the class trip because everybody else "works."

You can create a flower, a racecar, a dinosaur, the Statue of Liberty and the Eiffel Tower from JELL-O.

Potty training has taken over your life. Finally, your child decides to "do it." You are so overcome with joy by this major event that you invite your entire neighborhood over for the next performance.

You Know You've Been
A Stay-At-Home Mom Too Long When . . .

_____

Your childless friends are comparing the features of their high-end SUVs. You are gushing over all of the bells and whistles on your new Exersaucer.

* * * * *

You know every make and model of your son's 400-plus Matchbox car collection.

The only meaningful conversations you have are with the nurses at the Poison Control Center.

• • • • •

You're at home, actually accomplishing some minor chore and you think, "O.K., how long can I let him swing in that contraption without causing brain damage?"

You Know You've Been
A Stay-At-Home Mom Too Long When . . .

At the end of a tough day, you cave in at the convenience store and buy your child a Slurpee the size of Lake Okeechobie.

**You Know You've Been
A Stay-At-Home Mom Too Long When . . .**

_____

You've had so many playdates at YOUR house, you know all of the idiosyncracies of every kid on the block:

a. Cut Mikey's food in triangles.

b. Sam will drink ONLY with a RED crazy straw.

c. Ben pees with the seat DOWN.

You Know You've Been
A Stay-At-Home Mom Too Long When . . .

YOU QUESTION WHETHER YOU CAN READ HIGHER THAN A FIRST GRADE LEVEL OR A BOOK WITHOUT A CAT IN THE HAT ON IT.

Your idea of dressing up is wearing lipstick to match the jelly stains on your wardrobe.

You tell the judge that selling your kids on e-Bay sounded like a good idea at the time.

You Know You've Been
A Stay-At-Home Mom Too Long When . . .

Your single friend calls. You are going to strangle yourself with the phone cord when she asks, "So, how is your retirement lifestyle going?"

After ten months of nursing, you realize your two former perky "balloons" have deflated, NEVER to be full-blown again.

You Know You've Been
A Stay-At-Home Mom Too Long When . . .

POP QUIZ #2

Your life as a stay-at-home mom would be greatly enhanced if you left your kids at home so you could:

1.   Vacation at an expensive spa.
2.   Take a second honeymoon in Hawaii with your spouse.
3.   Join the Federal Witness Protection program.

You are reading a parenting magazine, and you come upon an article describing the qualities of perfect parents. You realize that you are:

1.   95% on the mark.
2.   Fair to middling.
3.   A candidate for immediate sterilization.

Your sixteen-year-old just got his driver's license. When you hand him the keys for the first time, you:

1.   Say, "Have fun!"
2.   Tell him that he must start paying his own auto insurance.
3.   Immediately double your dosage of Xanax.

Your child will leave for college soon. Your reaction to this is:

1.   A mixture of excitement and trepidation.
2.   Sheer anxiety and terror.
3.   To whip up a batch of daiquiris, crank up the stereo and do the Funky Chicken in anticipation of your impending freedom.

You Know You've Been
A Stay-At-Home Mom Too Long When . . .

A La Leche League member catches you giving a bottle to your infant and says, "I certainly hope that's breast milk!" You respond:

1. "Why yes, I just expressed it myself this morning."
2. "Want to taste?"
3. "Of course, with a little bourbon thrown in for some kick."

Having your children eat a balanced diet means:

1. Providing the proper amounts of foods containing proteins and carbohydrates as well as five fruits and vegetables each day.
2. A pizza with the works.
3. Oreo in one hand, chocolate chip in the other.
4. Alternating between Burger King and McDonald's every other day.

For you, a workout on the treadmill:

1. Hasn't happened since Dukakis ran for President.
2. Involves taking the clothes off it and hanging them up.
3. Is a metaphor for your life.

Missionaries come to your door and ring the bell. You:

1. Tell them you don't answer the door for anyone you don't know.
2. Take advantage of their kindness by getting them to watch your kids while you run to the market.
3. Say you're very interested in their "position" and ask if they would care to come in and demonstrate it.

You Know You've Been
A Stay-At-Home Mom Too Long When . . .

_____

Your mother-in-law comments on what a picky eater your child is. You respond by saying, "Not as picky as D.W." Your brain has deteriorated to a point where you cannot distinguish between the cartoon world and reality.

* * * * *

As a reflex, you turn to the dinner guest on your right and cut his steak into bite-sized pieces.

You Know You've Been
A Stay-At-Home Mom Too Long When . . .

_____

Your single friends are arguing who is cuter, Ben Affleck versus George Clooney. You butt in and ask, "Hey have any of you seen those hunky Kratt brothers from *Zoboomafoo*?"

You are too tired to formulate accurate responses to your kids' questions – for example, your five-year-old asks, "Why do skunks smell bad?" Your reply, "Poor hygiene."

You Know You've Been
A Stay-At-Home Mom Too Long When . . .

You're attached to that HUGE breast
pump. As you pump and pump for that
one ounce of milk, there's a word that
keeps entering your mind over and over
and over again...MOOOOOO!

You Know You've Been
A Stay-At-Home Mom Too Long When . . .

You're REALLY looking forward to the next PTA meeting.

Your child barfs so often, you've nicknamed her Mount Vesuvius.

A power lunch means inhaling a Big Mac while driving over 80 miles per hour to get to your kid's swim meet.

You Know You've Been
A Stay-At-Home Mom Too Long When . . .

YOU START TO TRADE POKÉMON CARDS WITH *YOUR* FRIENDS.

Your make-up routine has changed from mascara, eyeliner, blush, and lipstick to a nice, shiny coat of Chapstick.

Everyone raves about the butternut squash you serve at Thanksgiving dinner. You wonder, "Dare I tell them…it's Gerber's?"

You Know You've Been
A Stay-At-Home Mom Too Long When . . .

_____

You are finding that more and more, you are relying on your imaginary friends.

JUST TO SEE WHAT THE BIG ATTRACTION IS, YOU PUT A PIECE OF CORN UP YOUR NOSE.

Your mate would like to have sex tonight. You ask him, "What's the magic word?"

You Know You've Been
A Stay-At-Home Mom Too Long When . . .

Another new talent that you have
developed is driving with one hand on the
steering wheel while the other hand is
serving a three-course meal to your
back seat passengers.

You Know You've Been
A Stay-At-Home Mom Too Long When . . .

_____

You decide to treat yourself to new clothes. It's hard to decide between the gray warm-up suit or the navy.

* * * * *

Sprinkles have become the preferred topping for ice cream, yogurt, French toast, and meatloaf.

You Know You've Been
A Stay-At-Home Mom Too Long When . . .

_____

After your annual pap smear, as an automatic reflex, you ask the doctor if you can get a lollipop and a sticker.

• • • • •

Your idea of doing laps is walking back and forth in one-foot of peed-in baby pool water.

You Know You've Been
A Stay-At-Home Mom Too Long When . . .

You believe that the used breastpads that pop up all around your house would make a lovely set of coasters.

* * * * *

Dinner conversations with your mate used to be about current events, business affairs, and travel. Dinner conversations now include, hey, what dinner conversation??????

You Know You've Been
A Stay-At-Home Mom Too Long When . . .

You nurse your baby for more than six months; suddenly everybody becomes Freud and tries to analyze you.

Your working friends have invested in mutual funds while you're heavily invested in Brio trains.

The crumbs in your backpack now weigh a pound and a half.

You Know You've Been
A Stay-At-Home Mom Too Long When . . .

_____

AS YOU ARE RUSHING THROUGH
YET ANOTHER HECTIC MORNING
ROUTINE, YOU WONDER, "EXACTLY
HOW MANY DAYS CAN I GO
WITHOUT WASHING MY HAIR?"

*Your house looks as though
your decorator is the
Disney Store.*

The last time someone asked you when
you were going to go back to work, you
responded, "*@&%$#!!!"

You Know You've Been
A Stay-At-Home Mom Too Long When . . .

_____

The longest text you've read without interruption was inside of a fortune cookie.

You are no longer embarrassed to purchase items at the Dollar Store.

You are eternally grateful to the creator of...SWIM DIAPERS.

Someone at a cocktail party offers you something distasteful to eat. You cannot help but respond: "I would not eat them with a fox, I would not eat them in a box..."

• • • • •

YOUR BIGGEST AGGRAVATION: YOU'RE ALMOST AT THAT LAST PURPLE SQUARE IN CANDYLAND WHEN YOU PICK THE CARD THAT SENDS YOU TO THAT DAMN PLUMPY AGAIN!

You Know You've Been
A Stay-At-Home Mom Too Long When . . .

_____

POP QUIZ #3

Because you are financially limited due to one income, a meaningful cultural experience with your kids involves:

1. A trip to the library.
2. A trip to an Asian supermarket.
3. A trip to Alabama where you tell your kids you are in a foreign country.

In a desperate attempt to get your children's attention, you are reduced to:

1. Jumping up and down, screaming like a banshee.
2. Bribing them with a trip to Baskin Robbins.
3. Faking a seizure.

You tell your child that "flipping someone the bird" is:

1. Rude, childish and punishable by no dessert that night.
2. No way to solve one's differences.
3. Legally permitted ONLY by moms driving in minivans.

Your boys are infatuated with guns because:

1. Of the violence they've seen on T.V.
2. They instinctively know it will irritate you.
3. It's in their DNA.

You Know You've Been
A Stay-At-Home Mom Too Long When . . .

Your preteen daughter is hitting puberty and is rather hormonal:

1. You wish you hadn't waited until now to have that little chat.
2. You run to Home Depot to buy a huge padlock for her room until adolescence subsides.
3. Convinced that an alien life form has inhabited her body, you go looking in the basement for a pod.

The reason you became a parent in the first place is:

1. Because you love and adore children.
2. You wanted an excuse not to have to look for a job.
3. Contraceptive failure.

Your child begged for cello lessons. You ran out, rented a cello, hired a teacher, and now your child refuses to practice. You:

1. Nag him to practice.
2. Threaten to take away his Sony PlayStation privileges.
3. Bribe him with a dollar-a-day for each day of practice.
4. Take your child to the ER to have cello parts removed.

When the orthodontist gives you an estimate of what your child's braces will cost, you:

1. Decide this is a clear sign that you must now go back to work.
2. Pass around a collection plate at your family reunion.
3. Go on eBay to see if anyone wants to buy a kidney.

---

*You name your two new
puppies, Oprah and Dr. Phil.*

After your third child, you now have this
incredible ability to ignore clutter.

You are in such a fragile mental
state that you actually qualify
for "emotional handicap"
license plates.

You Know You've Been
A Stay-At-Home Mom Too Long When . . .

The first time you drop your child off at
preschool, when you walk out the doors
into the fresh air, you could swear you
hear a voice shouting, "Free at last, free
at last, great God Almighty, free at last!"

You Know You've Been
A Stay-At-Home Mom Too Long When . . .

_____

YOU WALK INTO THE LOCAL TOY STORE AND KNOW 95% OF THE MOMS SHOPPING. THE OTHER 5% LOOK FAMILIAR.

* * * * *

When someone offers you a cocktail, you ask for a Juicy Juice on the rocks.

You Know You've Been
A Stay-At-Home Mom Too Long When . . .

You get carpal tunnel not from typing but from changing diapers.

• • • • •

You have made a startling discovery. The tune from Twinkle, Twinkle, Little Star, Baa Baa Black Sheep, and the ABC song is the same.

You Know You've Been
A Stay-At-Home Mom Too Long When . . .

Your resumé lists your most valuable skill as being able to beat your 10-year-old in Donkey Kong.

You used to leave for your office with a spritz of Chanel No. 5. You now leave for the playground with a spritz of OFF.

YOU COULD HAVE A PH.D. IN GLUE STICK.

You Know You've Been
A Stay-At-Home Mom Too Long When . . .

At the end of each week, you add the MANY phone numbers of other desperate stay-at-home moms you picked up at the park to your phone directory.

* * * * *

A big accomplishment of the day is cutting UPC seals from a cereal box to get Tommy, Angelica and Chuckie dolls.

...And you *know* who Tommy, Angelica and Chuckie are!

You Know You've Been
A Stay-At-Home Mom Too Long When . . .

Your e-mail address is
poopydiapers@aol.com.

YOU START TO IDENTIFY WITH
THE STEPMOTHER WHO TRIES
TO LOSE THE KIDS IN *HANSEL
AND GRETEL.*

You know all the best bathrooms
in the best department stores in
the entire city to nurse your baby.

Your friend, a working mom, confides that she would love to switch places with you if she could. Her exact comment is, "I would love to be a stay-at-home mom, getting my nails done and going to the gym every day." After the paramedics peel her off the floor, you are able to resume your conversation.

You Know You've Been
A Stay-At-Home Mom Too Long When . . .

_____

*Friends drop in on you, the only drinks
you have to offer are apple juice and
chocolate milk in a box.*

You Know You've Been
A Stay-At-Home Mom Too Long When . . .

You have so many meals on the fly, you feel you could be a professional vending machine critic.

• • • • •

The amount of leftover food that goes down your garbage disposal each week could feed a third world country.

Saying your prayers, you thank the Lord for bringing Barney into this world.

* * * * *

Living on one income, you travel on a shoestring budget, staying in such cheap motels that they actually steal YOUR towels.

TIDYING UP THE HOUSE TO YOU MEANS STACKING UP ALL 100 FIREFIGHTER HELMETS NEATLY ON TOP OF EACH OTHER NEXT TO THE TIDY STACK OF 500 ART PROJECTS.

• • • • •

Your single friends are doing triathlons. Your version is giving the kids a bath, clipping their nails, and passing out.

You Know You've Been
A Stay-At-Home Mom Too Long When . . .

_____

The best love story you've seen in the last ten years... *SHREK!*

The insipid Wee Sing children's music that you can't stop humming makes you nostalgic for Muzak.

You can no longer afford haircuts in your expensive beauty salon. You now get your haircut at the same barber shop as your four-year-old causing you to resemble Jimmy Neutron.

**You Know You've Been
A Stay-At-Home Mom Too Long When . . .**

YOU HAVE TAKEN 34 BABY CLASSES INCLUDING *GYMBOREE, KINDERMUSIK*, AND *FUNFIT TOTS...* AND YOUR CHILD IS ONLY SEVEN MONTHS OLD.

• • • • •

Your husband asks you to pick a vacation - anywhere in the world. All you can come up with is Disneyland, Disney World, a Disney cruise or Eurodisney.

After years, you finally steal a moment
for a relaxing, hot bath. You have this
sudden urge to play with rubber duckies,
the Little Mermaid and write, "Please
help me," with your extra-supersized
soap crayons.

You Know You've Been
A Stay-At-Home Mom Too Long When . . .

You know every knock knock joke ever written.

TEN TIMES A DAY, YOU WALK INTO A ROOM AND FORGET WHY YOU WENT THERE.

One arm measures a good five inches longer than the other from carrying that damn "easy" carrier with a 20-pound baby inside.

In a crowded room, you can decipher the shriek of your child from those of your child's friends.

You're in bed. Your husband wants to know your fantasy. You reply, "going to Starbucks for a cup of coffee... ALONE."

You are designated signee for the neighborhood's Federal Express delivery packages.

You Know You've Been
A Stay-At-Home Mom Too Long When . . .

_____

The bright side of being constantly tethered to a gaggle of small children: you can pass gas in public and blame it on your kid's diaper.

• • • • •

You take a little extra time for yourself this morning, look in the mirror and think, "Hey, I look pretty good – maybe a little like Greta Van Susteren BEFORE the eye job."

You no longer have roots. You have two distinct colors of hair, black and blonde, of equal lengths.

You Know You've Been
A Stay-At-Home Mom Too Long When . . .

_____

Your friend tells you she plans to do the following when her firstborn arrives:

a. Use environmentally-friendly cloth diapers.
b. Limit T.V. to PBS for one-half hour per day.
c. Feed her child only healthy, organic foods and NO sweets.
d. Get her child to bed each night by 7:00 P.M.

You laugh so hard that you actually wet your pants.

You Know You've Been
A Stay-At-Home Mom Too Long When . . .

_____

POP QUIZ #4

If someone were to play you in a movie, it would be:

1. Carol Brady, oops, I mean Florence Henderson.
2. Sybil.
3. Kathy Bates.
4. Norman Bates.

A sacrifice to your child-free friends is: giving up massages. A sacrifice to you is:

1. Giving up coffee while pregnant.
2. Giving up alcohol while nursing.
3. What? I was supposed to give up alcohol while nursing?

A typical to-do list for you includes which of the following:

1. Buy milk and diapers.
2. Make brownies for school bake sale.
3. Empty bank account and run away from home.

You are no longer useful to your children because:

1. They can microwave their own T.V. dinners.
2. You cannot do any math beyond long division.
3. You forgot the recipe for Rice Krispie treats.

You Know You've Been
A Stay-At-Home Mom Too Long When . . .

_____

You are emotionally on the brink because:

1.   You are still suffering from postpartum depression even though your kids are teenagers.
2.   You forgot to take your Zoloft.
3.   Your husband announces he is going on a two-week business trip to Bermuda with his young, attractive secretary.

A romantic dinner with your spouse is:

1.   A picnic in a rustic setting.
2.   Going to a fancy French restaurant.
3.   Enjoying microwaved burritos and turning off the baby monitor while watching the Spice Channel.

Someone who works outside the home and has their kids in daycare asks you, "Don't you feel trapped?" You reply:

1.   "Absolutely not!"
2.   "No. (As you fight off the urge to gnaw at your leg)."
3.   "Let me out of this cage and I'll tell you."

From constantly being interrupted, you have attention deficit disorder and you can't remember:
1.   Anything before last Christmas.
2.   Anything discussed for more than 30 consecutive seconds.
3.

You Know You've Been
A Stay-At-Home Mom Too Long When . . .

YOU KNOW THE DIFFERENCE BETWEEN A BACKHOE AND A FRONT-END LOADER.

• • • • •

You put your ear up to an empty baby formula can and you swear you can actually hear Club Med.

You Know You've Been
A Stay-At-Home Mom Too Long When . . .

The only Emmy winner you recognized in the last five years has been Mr. Rogers.

You know that Sesame Street episode # 3940 is the one about the letter "C" and the number 12.

Sitting in the dentist's chair, having a root canal, you think, "At last, a relaxing getaway."

You Know You've Been
A Stay-At-Home Mom Too Long When . . .

You send your kids to Sunday school not so that they can get to know their Bible, but so you and your husband can get to "know" one other, Biblically speaking. ☺

• • • • •

Your child just projectile vomited green in your face. You wipe, continue your lunch, and think, "Now I know how the priest in the *Exorcist* felt."

You Know You've Been
A Stay-At-Home Mom Too Long When . . .

You try to sign your three-year-old up with your Schnauzer for obedience training.

Your new favorite singer: Raffi
Your new favorite instrumentalist: Raffi
Your new favorite song: anything by Raffi

Your old software collection: Quicken, Do-It-Yourself Wills, Williams-Sonoma Cookbook on CD-ROM. Your new software collection: Reader Rabbit, Green Eggs and Ham, Arthur's Birthday, and Pajama Sam.

You find yourself sitting in a fast-food
restaurant with a crown on your head.
You think, "I used to be respected
by people."

You Know You've Been
A Stay-At-Home Mom Too Long When . . .

_____

From washing your hands 100 times a day, one cannot tell the difference between your hands and the hands of your 96-year-old grandmother.

• • • • •

Your five-year-old starts to scribble with crayons – on your newly painted wall! You think, "Great! A project that will keep him busy for HOURS!"

You Know You've Been
A Stay-At-Home Mom Too Long When . . .

_____

The UPS man is shocked when you answer the door with your shirt half-open, breasts half-exposed. You nonchalantly say, "Why button up? He's going to eat again in a half-hour."

ANOTHER STAY-AT-HOMER ASKS, "DO YOU WANT TO GO OUT ONE EVENING – NO KIDS, NO HUSBANDS?" YOUR RESPONSE TIME IS A RECORD .00001 NANOSECOND.

**You Know You've Been
A Stay-At-Home Mom Too Long When . . .**

In a neighborhood game of hide-and-seek, you go hide at the corner pub.

YOUR CHILD'S BEST SIT-DOWN
MEAL OF THE DAY IS IN
YOUR MINIVAN.

You are listed as the "emergency contact" for half of the children in your kid's school.

You Know You've Been
A Stay-At-Home Mom Too Long When . . .

_____

You receive a telemarketing call during dinner and you are thrilled...ADULT CONVERSATION!

• • • • •

You're in a room full of toddlers. Someone stinks. You know it's not yours without even doing the "nose-in-tush" move.

You Know You've Been
A Stay-At-Home Mom Too Long When . . .

You realize that there has to be something in between attending PTA meetings and being eligible for Medicare.

* * * * *

Towards the end of a fancy dinner party, you look at your husband and blurt out, "Honey, this is the five-minute warning."

You Know You've Been
A Stay-At-Home Mom Too Long When . . .

You know the real names of Barney's friends. You know that Barney's friends HAVE real names.

Your sex life couldn't even get a PG-13 rating.

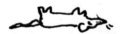

You indulge your child's every whim, including one where you permit her to have a wake and a viewing for her dead gerbil.

You Know You've Been
A Stay-At-Home Mom Too Long When . . .

You've taken 28 books out of the library. They all RHYME.

You think the Teletubbies are speaking perfect English. (If this one is true, you must return to work *immediately!*)

YOUR ANNUAL HOLIDAY LETTER TO FRIENDS AND FAMILY CITES YOUR MAIN FEAT FOR THE YEAR ...A BASKET YOU MADE ENTIRELY FROM POPSICLE STICKS.

Tools of your trade: crayons, blocks,
glue, pipe cleaners, beads, glitter,
and martinis.

You Know You've Been
A Stay-At-Home Mom Too Long When . . .

————————————

You realize that if you wait until your kids are in college to apply for a job, you will be at the mandatory retirement age of most employers.

• • • • •

You are so out of touch with reality, you are not sure whether the following are still alive: Milton Berle, Jerry Lewis, Gerald Ford or any member of the Beach Boys or Lynrd Skynrd.

You Know You've Been
A Stay-At-Home Mom Too Long When . . .

You get tons of fulfillment from taking a stubborn booger out of your child's nose (same uplifting feeling from earwax).

* * * * *

The last time you worked on office equipment, it was on an IBM Selectric with one of those fast-moving balls.

You Know You've Been
A Stay-At-Home Mom Too Long When . . .

YOU FIND YOU'RE REPEATING
YOURSELF OVER AND OVER.

YOU FIND YOU'RE REPEATING
YOURSELF OVER AND OVER.

You and your five-year old both laugh
hysterically at the fact that the
number 3, when turned on it's side,
does, indeed, look like a tushy.

For vicarious thrills, you spend significant
amounts of time eavesdropping on your
neighbor's phone conversation picked up
by your baby monitor.

You Know You've Been
A Stay-At-Home Mom Too Long When . . .

The magazines you used to subscribe to were: Cosmo, Time, and Gourmet; the magazines you now subscribe to are Parents, Family Fun, and Highlights.

* * * * *

You can prepare breakfast, eat, skim the paper, pay bills, scrub the kitchen counters, sweep the floor, have a phone conversation - all with a baby attached to your nipple.

You Know You've Been
A Stay-At-Home Mom Too Long When . . .

_____

YOUR NEW WARDROBE USED TO COME FROM BLOOMINGDALE'S AND MACY'S. YOUR NEW WARDROBE NOW COMES FROM, HEY, WHAT NEW WARDROBE?

• • • • •

Your child wins a twelve-cent goldfish at the county fair. You immediately go to PetSmart and spend $124.90 on life-sustaining goldfish equipment. The fish dies anyway.

You Know You've Been
A Stay-At-Home Mom Too Long When . . .

―――――――――

For outings, you pack snacks, change
of clothes, cell phone, plastic bags,
wipes, disposable camera, Bandaids,
crayons, lollypops (for emergency
use). When your husband takes the
kids on an outing, he packs –
NOTHING!

* * * * *

A parent-teacher conference
is considered the best
get-together of the year.

You Know You've Been
A Stay-At-Home Mom Too Long When . . .

YOUR FRIEND PHONES TO
TELL YOU SHE IS ENGAGED
WHEREUPON YOU SAY,
"THAT'S NICE" AND ASK
YOUR THREE-YEAR-OLD IF HE
NEEDS TO BE WIPED.

• • • • •

You look forward to a dinner date with your husband, not for the adult companionship, not for the adult food...just so you don't have to wear a nursing bra.

You Know You've Been
A Stay-At-Home Mom Too Long When . . .

_____

Exotic cuisine to you is pizza WITH
a topping.

You know the recipe
for Play-Doh by heart.

You think nothing of driving your child to the
bus stop in a housecoat looking like a
hurricane victim.

You Know You've Been
A Stay-At-Home Mom Too Long When . . .

———————————

You own several pairs of crotchless panties – not to spice up your sex life, but because you haven't made it to the underwear department in three years.

The last time you read the whole paper, O.J. was in the headlines.

Your only regular exercise for the past year has been intense Kegels.

You Know You've Been
A Stay-At-Home Mom Too Long When . . .

Your husband's fantasy of you is not in a French Maid costume but of you in a business suit with a paycheck in hand.

Neither you nor your 9-year-old have slept through the night in 9 years.

You have to go back to work just so you will **STOP SHOPPING!**

You Know You've Been
A Stay-At-Home Mom Too Long When . . .

LAST POP QUIZ!

From being out of the work force for so long, you fear that:

1.   Your husband will never be able to retire.
2.   Your kids will not be able to attend a private college.
3.   During your golden years, you will be "dumpster diving."

You think you are looking pretty good these days when:

1.   The black rings under your eyes have faded to a nice shade of gray.
2.   The elephant-like skin on your stomach jiggles only when you laugh.
3.   Your breast-feeding boobs now hang above your belly button.
4.   All of the above.

It's dinnertime and you hear the damn ice cream truck jingle. You:

1.   Immediately start singing Jingle Bells at the top of your lungs.
2.   Tell your kids you will buy them ice cream only if they eat it *after* their meal.
3.   Buy them their $3 Popsicle dinner.

You know that The Wiggles are a:

1.   Children's musical group.
2.   Fruity snake-like snack.
3.   Newly discovered contagious disease.
4.   Hot sex toy.

You Know You've Been
A Stay-At-Home Mom Too Long When . . .

_____

You've been a full-time stay-at-home mom for many, many years. You're getting the feeling it may be time to return to work. Here are some clues that should help you reach your decision...

YOU KNOW IT'S TIME TO GO BACK TO WORK WHEN...

Your child has a full-length beard.

Your friends are looking at retirement communities.

You have totally run out of conversation that any normal person over the age of five would be interested in.

Your child hands you the "Want Ads."

You have a HUGE crush on Bob from Sesame Street.

You have not bought yourself a new outfit in 16 years.

The entire PTA is begging you NOT to run for president again.

The style of clothing that you used to wear to work is back in style – for the third time.

You're expecting your second...GRANDCHILD.

Your shopping list item of DIAPERS has been replaced by DEPENDS.

About The Authors

Janice Haas grew up in Brooklyn, New York, where you must be funny to survive. She migrated south, now residing in Bethesda, Maryland, with her husband, David and their two awesome boys, Evan and Jacob. Janice has written humor articles for the newspaper, *Washington Jewish Week*. This is her first book.

Sally Pessin grew up in Stamford, Connecticut, in a neighborhood full of stay-at-home moms. An attorney by training and former stand-up comic, Sally has a home-based humorous, personalized poetry company called *Washington Wordsmiths*. Sally resides in Bethesda, Maryland, with her husband, Andy, and her wonderful son, Eric, whom she has been at home with since his birth.

About The Illustrator

Annette Abrams is a stay-at-home mom who draws and teaches preschool when her kids are not home. She lives in Bethesda, Maryland, with her husband, those three great kids, cat and dog.

TO ORDER COPIES OF:
You Know You've Been A Stay-At-Home Mom too long when . . . . .

Please send me _____ copies at $7.95 each plus $2.00 S/H each. (Make checks payable to **QUIXOTE PRESS.**)

Name _____

Street _____

City _____ State _____ Zip _____

SEND ORDERS TO:
QUIXOTE PRESS
1854-345th Avenue
Wever IA   52658
800-571-2665

TO ORDER COPIES OF:
You Know You've Been A Stay-At-Home Mom too long when . . . . .

Please send me _____ copies at $7.95 each plus $2.00 S/H each. (Make checks payable to **QUIXOTE PRESS.**)

Name _____

Street _____

City _____ State _____ Zip _____

SEND ORDERS TO:
QUIXOTE PRESS
1854-345th Avenue
Wever IA   52658
800-571-2665